More Good Thoughts from Good People
PRAY TO LOVE
LOVE TO PRAY

Prayers, Reflections, and Life Stories of 15 Great Pray-ers

Biographical Sketches & Prayer Selections
by Carol Graser

HI-TIME Publishing
Milwaukee, WI 53222-2136

When you call me, when you pray to me, I will listen to you. When you look for me, you will find me. Yes, when you seek me with all your heart, you will find me with you, says the Lord ....

Jeremiah 29:12-14

Cover design by William J. Schueller
Interior art and design by Patricia A. Lynch

Scripture texts used in this work are taken from *The New American Bible*
©1970 by the Confraternity of Christian Doctrine, Washington, DC, and
are used with permission. All rights reserved.

©1998 Carol A. Graser
HI-TIME Publishing
330 Progress Road
Dayton, OH 45449
800-558-2292

ISBN 0-937997-43-9

CONTENTS

*Reference numbers within the text refer to acknowledgments.

There are different gifts but the same Spirit; there are different ministries but the same Lord; there are different works but the same God who accomplishes all of them in everyone.

1 Corinthians 12:4-6

When we hear these familiar words of the Apostle Paul, we may think of traditional ministries such as teaching, preaching, healing, prophesying. But could we envision the gifts or ministries of a shepherd, a chancellor of a powerful nation, a pioneering educator, a veteran of World War I, an eccentric artist, a Midwest farmgirl, and children of the rich and famous?

The short biographies, prayers, and reflections in *More Pray To Love, Love To Pray* celebrate the diversity of the Christian family and draw us closer to the source of our unity, a unity that triumphs over all human divisions, that transcends time, place, and circumstance. It is the one Spirit who moves every one of us to search, to listen, to be honest, generous, and open, and, in the words of C.S. Lewis "... to forever know and praise some one aspect of the divine beauty better than any other creature can ...."

We might well wonder how we are called to know and praise God better than any other creature. In listening in on the intimate conversations of the men and women who pray in these pages, we can recognize the unique gifts we have been given and invite the Spirit to move anew in our words and actions. And we can pray with Black Elk who said, "We should come to understand well that all things are the works of the Great Spirit .... When we understand this deeply in our hearts, then we will all fear and love and know the Great Spirit; then we will be and act and live as God intends."

PATRICK OF IRELAND

389 - 461
Feast Day - March 17

"Will the real St. Patrick please stand up?" Giving an accurate account of the life of the "Apostle of the Irish" has never been easy because over the years the few historical facts available have often been colored and enhanced by many stories and legends.

We know that Patricius, the son of a well-to-do landowner, was born in Roman-occupied Britain. Some sixteen years after his birth, invading Anglo-Saxons pillaged and destroyed his father's estate, kidnapped the young son, and carried him off to pagan Ireland to serve as a herdsman slave. For six years, obeying orders, serving others, and tending sheep made Patrick, as he came to be known, a self-effacing, prayerful, and generous man.

At twenty-two, longing to return to his homeland and feeling a call to the priesthood, Patrick escaped his captors and fled back to Britain. There, motivated by his dream to return to Ireland to convert the people to Christianity, he prayed and studied and was eventually ordained. During the next several years, Patrick served the Church in Britain. In 432, as a consecrated bishop, he received permission to return to Ireland. Together with other missionaries who preceded him or came later, he faced the enormous challenge of bringing the Word to a "heathen people."

Much of the story of Ireland's conversion to the Christian faith is a blend of fact and fiction. Did Patrick really drive the snakes out of the land? Did he use a shamrock to teach the people about the Trinity? Did he live to be 120, and does he still sing alleluias in the Irish hills every Easter eve? Not very likely. Yet the fact remains that within a little more than a decade Patrick and others made Ireland "a bright star in the firmament of the Church." The greatest sermon Patrick ever preached was his own life.

5

PRAYERS & REFLECTIONS

Morning Prayer

I arise today strengthened by beholding the heavens —
    the warmth of the sun and glow of the moon,
    the speed of lightning flashing across the sky ....

I arise today strengthened by praying
    to you, O God, Father, Son and Holy Spirit —
    three-in-one Creator of Creation.

With your abiding help and grace,
    I place the heavens, all of creation, and this day
    in your hands, O Creator of Creation!

In God's Care

O Lord, my God and Father,
    you have watched over me even before I knew you,
    and before I was able to distinguish right from wrong.
    You have guarded and comforted me as your child ....
    I believe that I have been sustained by Christ my Lord,
    and by your Spirit crying out in my behalf.[1]

Response

Lord Jesus, my God, if I am worthy,
    I am ready to give up my life,
without hesitation and most willingly,
    for your holy name![1]

With God's Help

May the strength of God pilot us.
    May the power of God preserve us.
May the wisdom of God instruct us.
    May the hand of God protect us.
May the way of God direct us.
    May the shield of God defend us.[2]

Christ, My Strength, My Life

Christ beside me,
    Christ before me,
        Christ behind me.

Christ within me,
    Christ beneath me,
        Christ above me.

Christ on my right hand,
    Christ on my left,
        Christ where I lie,
            Christ where I sit,
                Christ where I rise.

Christ in the hearts of all who think of me,
Christ in the mouths of all who speak to me,
Christ in every eye that sees me,
Christ in every ear that hears me!

— attributed to St. Patrick

Doing the Lord's Work

From the time I came to know God,
his love and the fear of him have grown in me,
and up to now — thanks to the grace of God —
I have kept the faith![1]

For the unspeakable glory of life everlasting
which is in Christ our Lord,
I am a servant in him to strangers and unbelievers.[1]

To strengthen and confirm our faith,
let us strive for greater things and try to do better![1]

Without doubt, on the last day,
we shall rise in the brightness of the sun,
that is, in the glory of Christ Jesus our Redeemer,
as children of the living God and joint heirs with Christ![1]

BERNARD OF CLAIRVAUX

1090 - 1153
Father and Doctor of the Church
Feast Day - August 20

Bernard of Clairvaux was a man on the move and, it must be said, something of a Pied Piper. This mighty voice of the twelfth century had little time for small talk, indecision, or frivolity. "Life is short," he often seemed to be saying, "and I have worlds to conquer for the Lord."

Born into a family of nobility and wealth near Dijon, France, Bernard determined at an early age to dedicate his life to God. When he was twenty-two, he entered the Cistercian monastery at Citeaux, and brought with him thirty of his relatives and friends! Less than two years later he was sent to establish a monastery at Clairvaux, and within a short time was made its abbot. Clairvaux soon became a center for prayer and penance, for learning and scholarship.

Because of his holiness, prayerfulness, and remarkable leadership ability, Bernard was often called upon to serve the Church as preacher, scholar, and organizer. Bishops, kings, and popes sought his advice. When schisms and heresies arose within the Church, he traveled throughout Europe, teaching, encouraging prayer and penance, and restoring peace and unity.

A prolific writer, Bernard left a body of spiritual works that has continued to influence saints, scholars, and the rest of us throughout the centuries. Best of all, wherever he went, whatever he did, this charismatic monk inspired others to lives of prayerfulness and loving service to the Lord.

PRAYERS & REFLECTIONS

A Child Is Given Us

Before you came into this world, Lord,
your love was hidden from us.
Your mercy was but the object of a promise,
not of an experience.

But now, Lord,
may we believe in what we see —
a little child is given us.
In him lies the fullness of divinity.

What great proof of your love you have given us,
adding to your humanity the name of God!

All About Love

Love is sufficient of itself;
it gives pleasure by itself and because of itself.
Love is its own merit, its own reward.

Love looks for no cause outside itself,
no effect beyond itself.
Its profit lies in its practice ....

When God loves, all he desires
is to be loved in return.
The sole purpose of God's love is to be loved,
in the knowledge that those who love him
are made happy by their love of him.

Memorare to Our Lady

Remember, O most gracious Virgin Mary,
that never was it known
that anyone who fled to your protection,
implored your help or sought your intercession,
was left unaided.
Inspired by this confidence, I fly unto you,
O virgin of virgins, my mother.
To you I come, before you I stand, sinful and sorrowful.
O mother of the Word Incarnate,
despise not my petitions, but in your mercy,
hear and answer me. Amen.

A Word to the Wise

Do not believe everything you hear;
Do not judge everything you see;
Do not do everything you can;
Do not give everything you have;
Do not say everything you know.
Pray, read, withdraw, be silent, be at peace!

Plan Ahead

We give only from our surplus —
if you would be wise,
make yourself a reservoir
before becoming a channel.

The Way to Confidence

Return to your own self —
enter into your heart.
Learn the value of your soul —
ponder what you were, are,
should have been, and can be.

What Lies Ahead

Death, than which there is nothing more certain.
Judgment, than which there is nothing more strict.
Hell, than which there is nothing more terrible.
Heaven, than which there is nothing more delightful!

The Way to Peace

Let us learn to cast our hearts unto God.

Prayer is a wine which makes glad the heart of all!

Go, ask Mary for help and you will be saved.

We cannot begin to imagine the capacity for love
that the soul will have in the next life,
nor even what the capacity is in this present life!

CLARE OF ASSISI

1194 - 1253
Feast Day - August 11

A good friendship can change the entire course of a person's life. This was the case with Clare Offreduccio, a beautiful and well-to-do young woman from the town of Assisi in Italy. Although the pampered Clare enjoyed the "good life" with family and friends, she was often bored and restless for something more.

Then, one evening a relative took Clare to a nearby church to hear a talk by a dynamic young speaker, Francis Bernardone from Assisi. After that first encounter, Clare and Francis became good friends. Under his guidance, she began to understand her own restlessness and became more and more determined to renounce her riches and dedicate her life entirely to God.

To the surprise and, in some cases, the dismay of family and friends, the young woman vowed her life to God, received a religious habit from Francis, and established a convent at San Damiano. In the years that followed, with continued counsel from her friend, Clare established convents throughout Europe. Because the two insisted upon the strict practice of poverty and austerity within the order, the new community of women came to be known as "Poor Clares."

An effective and well-loved superior, Clare guided and led her community with prayerfulness, kindness, and good humor. She was strict, but always gently so. During her almost thirty years as a religious, she suffered greatly from poor health but was never too ill to serve others. Her fame as a deeply spiritual and down-to-earth woman spread rapidly throughout medieval Europe. She died in 1253 and was canonized only two years later.

PRAYERS & REFLECTIONS

I Will Remember

Jesus Savior, from your position on the cross,
you warned us to consider carefully
these acts of love:
"All you who pass this way,
behold and see if there is sorrow like mine."

Help me, Lord, to answer your cries
with one voice and one spirit:
Jesus, I will be mindful and remember.
All praise and thanksgiving to you forever.
Amen.

Prayer for Constancy

I pray, Lord Jesus, that having redeemed me
by your suffering on the cross,
you will deliver me from all evils,
past, present, and to come.
By your unthinkable death, please give me
a lively faith, a firm hope, and an enduring love,
so that I may consistently serve you
with all my heart, all my soul, and all my strength.

Please make me firm and steadfast
in loving service to others,
and grant me perseverance in following you,
so that I may be able to please you always.
Amen.

To the Giver of Life

Blessed are you, my Lord God,
for creating me and giving me life;
and by your death on the cross
blessed are you, my Jesus,
for redeeming me and giving me *eternal* life!

Mirror

Jesus is an unclouded mirror for us:
Look at him as he is laid in a manger
   and wrapped in swaddling clothes —
what marvelous humility and poverty of spirit.
The King of angels and Lord of heaven and earth,
   resting in a poor manger!

Look at the many sufferings Jesus endured
   to redeem the human race —
In the depths of this mirror,
consider the unspeakable love which caused him
   to suffer on the wood of the cross
and to endure the most shameful kind of death.

Truly, our Savior is the "splendor of eternal glory,
   the brightness of eternal light,
      a mirror without cloud."
Let us look deeply into that mirror.
      Let us thank him!

A Steady Course

As we set out on the path of the Lord,
let us take care that we do not turn away from it.[1]

The Road Ahead

What you hold, may you always hold.
What you do, may you always do and never abandon,
but with swift pace, light step and unswerving feet,
so that even your steps stir up no dust.
Go forward
securely, joyfully, swiftly,
on the path of *prudent* happiness![1]

Blueprint for Happiness

If you suffer with Christ, you will reign with him.
If you weep with Christ, you will rejoice with him.

Live and hope in the Lord,
and let your service be according to reason.

Love him totally
who gave himself totally for your love!

Our labor here is brief,
but the reward is *eternal.*

THOMAS MORE

1477 - 1535
Feast Day - June 22

L ong before 1529, when Thomas More was appointed Lord Chancellor of England, he knew that trouble was brewing. A friend of King Henry VIII's for many years, More had served the monarch faithfully through troublesome times within and without the Catholic Church. Henry, who years before had earned the title "Defender of the Faith," now had his own agenda, which included divorce, remarriage, repudiation of papal authority, and declaration of himself as head of the Church of England.

More's private life had always been comparatively peaceful, serene, and quite ordinary. Educated in law at Oxford, he was a well-known and well-liked scholar and reformer, a writer, wit, and political satirist. Most important, he was an ardent and prayerful Catholic and a devoted husband and family man — truly a "man for all seasons."

Then in 1534, because More had taken a strong stand against Henry's self-serving policies and had resigned as Chancellor, he was in deep trouble. The final straw came when he refused to sign Henry's Act of Supremacy. For this courageous stand, he was imprisoned in the Tower of London and sentenced to death. Before his execution, he wrote a letter to his daughter Margaret. His words reveal the kind of man he was: "Do not let your mind be troubled .... Nothing can come but what God wills. I am sure that whatever that may be, it shall indeed be the best .... Pray for me, dear Meg, and I shall pray for thee, that we may merrily meet in heaven!"

And so, Thomas More's story has a *happy* ending.

PRAYERS & REFLECTIONS

Prayer for Every Day

Give me, good Lord,
a humble, lowly, quiet, peaceable, patient,
charitable, kind and filial and tender mind —
every shade, in fact, of charity;
with all my words and all my works,
and all my thoughts —
to have a taste of your truly blessed Spirit![1]

The Best of Partnerships

Grant me the grace, good Lord,
gladly to think of you,
earnestly to call for your help,
busily to love you more and more,
continually to have you in mind,
ceaselessly to recall the death you suffered for me,
consistently to give you my *deepest* thanks.
Amen.

Lord, give me patience in tribulation and grace in
everything to conform my will to you,
that I may truly say:
"Your will be done, on earth as it is in heaven."[1]

The things, good Lord, that I pray for,
give me your grace to labor for![1]

Help in the Storm

I will trust in the Lord,
though I feel myself weakening
and on the verge of being overcome with fear.
I shall remember how St. Peter, at a blast of wind,
began to sink because of his lack of faith,
and I shall do as he did —
call upon Christ and pray to him for help.
And then, I trust that Jesus will place his hand on me
and in the stormy seas hold me from drowning!

Faith Matters

Comfort in times of trouble
can be secured only on the sure ground of faith.

God has faithfully promised
to protect and defend
those who faithfully dwell in the trust of his help.[2]

If I am distracted,
Holy Communion helps me to become recollected ....
I arm myself for the day's cares and concerns
by receiving the Eucharist.

What people call fame is, after all,
a very *windy* thing!

I right heartily pray all of you to serve God
and to be merry and rejoice in him.[2]

When the Going Gets Tough ...

The martyrs who freely and eagerly faced death
because of their faith in Christ
are especially worthy of the laurels of triumph
because, with a joy that left no room for sorrow,
they betrayed no trace of sadness or fear ....[2]

The Tough Get Going!

Yet we cannot deny the triumph
of those who do not rush forward of their own accord,
but nevertheless do not hang back or withdraw
once they face adversity —
but rather, *go on in spite of fearful anxiety*
and face the terrible prospect
out of love for Christ.[2]

RICHARD CRASHAW

1612 - 1649

Many people have never heard of Richard Crashaw. "Richard who?" they ask. Richard Crashaw, a poet and priest of the post-Elizabethan period in England, was a deeply spiritual thinker who wrote powerful reflections on religious themes.

Little is known of Crashaw's personal life. The only son of a Puritan preacher with stridently anti-Catholic views, he had a lonely childhood — his mother and stepmother both died before he was nine. His was a classical education, first at Pembroke College and later at Cambridge. He was greatly influenced by Roman Catholic teachings, Renaissance music and art, and, in a very special way, by the writings, teachings, and example of the newly canonized Teresa of Avila.

Soon after his conversion to Catholicism, Crashaw studied for the priesthood and was ordained. Because of his Roman Catholic and royalist sympathies, he had few friends in London. After a trip to Rome, he found employment in the household of Cardinal Palotta. Eventually, he was appointed a canon of the Church of Our Lady of Loretto. He died there a few months later and is buried there.

Throughout these later years especially, Crashaw wrote poetry that expresses his love for Christ and Mary and the saints. Along with John Donne, Andrew Marvell, and George Herbert, he is considered one of the great metaphysical poets of his time. Some persons may find the elaborate and subtle metaphors and flowery language of these poets excessive, but their works have withstood the test of time and have provided prayerful moments for people of all times, all ages.

PRAYERS & REFLECTIONS

Motto

Live, Jesus, live, and let it be
my life to die for love of thee!

The Cross of Jesus

Tall tree of life, thy truth makes good
    what was till now not understood ....
         O my Savior, make me see
how dearly thou hast paid for me —
that lost again, my life may prove
as then in death, so now in love.

Recommendation

These hours, and those which hover over my end,
into thy hands and heart, Lord, I commend.

Take both to thy account, that I and mine
in that hour, and in these, may all be thine.

That as I dedicate my devoutest breath
to make a kind of life for my Lord's death —

So from his living and life-giving death,
My dying life may draw a new and never fleeting breath.

To Our Blessed Lady in Heaven

Live, rosy princess, live.
And may the bright crown of incomparable light
Embrace thy radiant brow ....
Live, crown of women, queen of men.
Live, mistress of our song.
And when our weak desires have done their best —
Sweet angels, come, and sing the rest!

Christmas Wonder

Welcome all wonders in one night:
Eternity shut in a span,
summer in winter, day in night,
heaven on earth, and God in man —
Great-Little-One, whose all-embracing birth
lifts earth to heaven,
stoops heaven to earth!

Song of the Eucharist

Come, love, and let us work a song
loud and pleasant, sweet and long.
Let lips and hearts lift high the noise
of so just and solemn joys ....

Lo, the life-food of angels then
bowed to the lowly lives of men ....
Jesus master, just and true —
our food and faithful shepherd, too!

RICHARD CRASHAW

Hope: A True Companion

Dear hope! Earth's dowry, and heaven's debt,
    the entity of things that are not yet ....
Faith's sister! Nurse of fair desire —
    fear's antidote — a wise and well-stayed fire.

Dear Friend's Death

Angels, thy old friends, shall greet thee,
glad at their own home now to meet thee!

MARY THERESA OF JESUS GERHARDINGER

1797 - 1879
Feast Day - May 9

Caroline Gerhardinger was born into a well-to-do and fervently Catholic family in suburban Bavaria, but when she was growing up, the Napoleonic Wars and the Age of Enlightenment were taking their toll on the religious lives of all Germans. Many schools had been closed and Christian education forbidden. Advanced schooling for young women was considered frivolous and unnecessary.

Caroline's spiritual advisor, Father George M. Wittmann, was convinced that education of Catholic girls and young women was of prime importance, not only for the welfare of family life but also for the life of the Church in Germany. Under Father Wittmann's guidance, with encouragement from her parents, and after much prayer, Caroline came to recognize her calling not only as an educator but also as the founder of a religious community especially dedicated to the Christian education of girls and young women.

In 1833, Caroline established the School Sisters of Notre Dame. As Mother Mary Theresa of Jesus, she oversaw the development of a Catholic educational system, first in Germany and then throughout Europe. In 1847, she accompanied four sisters to the United States to help with the establishment of schools in the eastern part of the country. With the great patron of the parochial system, Father John Neumann, she traveled as far west as Wisconsin, investigating possibilities of future schools.

Always led by the Spirit and unafraid to start new ventures, Mother Mary Theresa was a woman of courage and trust. Until her death at the motherhouse in Munich, she continued to be a "hands-on" leader deeply involved in doing God's work. She was beatified in 1985 by Pope John Paul II.

PRAYERS & REFLECTIONS

Sparks

Earnestly desiring to love God
is striking a spark from flint;
doing God's will is feeding the fire:

I cannot love you, O God,
if I do not conform my will to yours,
if I do not become again a *spark* for you,
a spark aglow with you,
because to do your will is to love you![1]

Prayer with Heart

O God,

In prayer we experience
that you have a heart for us.
When we pray in the right way —
only when we have a heart for one another —
are we truly human.

O God,

Prayer and life hang together.
Let us *live* our prayers![2]

In God's Time

All the works of God
proceed slowly and in pain;
but then, their roots are all the sturdier,
and their flowering all the lovelier.[1]

Our goal is God because he alone
is the reason for our existence.[2]

If the dear Lord wants to call something into life,
he also gives the means for that to happen.[2]

Where there is no human help,
God's help is still possible.[2]

The Lord of all hearts, of heaven and earth,
knows *exactly*
when the oil in the jar and the flour in the bin
are coming to an end![2]

The Lord is our protector, our helper,
and one day will also be our immense reward in heaven,
where we hope to see each other again,
forever to praise the Lord,
who has shown us such great mercy.[2]

Follow the Star

Follow the star which has arisen in you —
it will certainly lead you to Jesus.[2]

The candle consumes itself
as it serves others by its shining.[2]

No angel is able to count the blessings
which, even on a single day,
God gives to each person.[2]

Prayer is for us the ladder,
the key, and the gate to heaven![2]

BLACK ELK

1863 - 1950

Black Elk was a priest of the Oglala Sioux Indians. He knew and practiced the Native American seven rites of the sacred pipe, and he felt always that his purpose in life was to teach his people how to come to terms with God, other persons, and nature.

Black Elk's life spans pivotal events in Native American history. A relative of the famous Chief Crazy Horse, he was born along the Powder River in Wyoming. During his childhood and early manhood, he saw his tribe transformed from buffalo-hunting warriors roaming the Great Plains to poverty-stricken prisoners confined to thirteen government reservations. When he was only nine, he experienced a vision in which he was given powers "to bring to life the flowering tree of his people."

In 1876 at age thirteen, the very young warrior actually fought at the Battle of the Little Bighorn. In the years that followed, he witnessed the consequences of Indian resistance.

Black Elk's first encounter with Catholic missionaries occurred in 1889 in South Dakota. Feeling that he could help his people best by becoming a Christian, he was converted. After the U.S. Army's horrendous massacre of nonwarrior Indians at Wounded Knee, South Dakota, Black Elk became more and more active in assisting the Jesuits and other missionaries with teaching Indians the Gospel message of peace. But, as before, he also continued "to bring to life the flowering tree" by giving new life to the ancient rites of the Oglala Sioux.

When Black Elk died in 1950, he was holding a rosary and a Lakota pipe. His daughter, Lucy Looks-Twice, a devout Catholic, related later that he always believed that lights in the sky would accompany his death. The night Black Elk died, the area where he lived experienced an unusually bright meteor shower.

BLACK ELK

PRAYERS & REFLECTIONS

To the Creator

Hey, hey! Hey, hey! Hey, hey!
Great Spirit, you have been always,
    and before you no one has been ....
Everything has been made by you.
The star nations all over the universe
        you have finished,
  The four quarters of the earth
      you have finished.
  The day, and in that day — everything
      you have finished!

Grandfather, Great Spirit, lean close to the earth —
        hear the voice I send ....
  You where the sun shines continually, and
        where comes the daybreak star and the day,
            behold me.
  You where the summer lives,
            behold me.
  And you, Mother Earth,
      show mercy to your children ....

Hear me, four quarters of the world —
      a relative I am:
Give me the strength to walk the soft earth,
      a relative to all that is.
Give me the eyes to see, the strength to understand,
      so that I may be like you.
With your power, I can face the winds!
      Amen.[1]

[Morning Prayer]

O Morning Star, there at the place
        where the sun comes up,
O you who have the wisdom we seek, help us ....
   so that generations to come will have Light
       as they walk the sacred path.

O Great Spirit, we give thanks for the Light
       which you have given to us
through the Power of the place where the sun comes up.
   Help us, O Power of the east.
       Be merciful to us.[2]

For God's Help

Great Spirit, my Grandfather, hear my feeble voice.
You have said that I should make the tree to bloom.
       With tears running, I must say
       that the tree has never bloomed —
       where I stand the tree is withered,
   and I remember the great vision you gave me.
   It may be that a root of the sacred tree still lives.
       Nourish it, then, that it may leaf and bloom
          and be filled with singing birds.
Hear me, Great Spirit, that our people may again find
       the good road
       and a shielding tree. Amen.[1]

[Gifts from God]

The heavens are sacred,
for it is there that the Great Spirit lives;
the heavens are a cloak for God's universe.[2]

The eagle soars above my head
and flutters there;
suddenly the sky is full of friendly wings
all coming toward me.[1]

The waters of the sky and earth are from God —
Remember the One who guards these
and the sanctity of all things ....
When you finish drinking the water of life,
raise your hand in thanks
to the Power of the place
where the sun goes down![2]

[The food given to you by the Great Spirit]
... will become your body and soul....
As He is merciful to you,
so you too must be merciful to others!

— based on material in *The Sacred Pipe*

What Unites Us

There is much talk of peace among Christians ....
Perhaps it may be, and this is my prayer that ....
peace may come
to all people who can understand,
and come to realize in their hearts
that we Indians know the One true God,
and that we pray to God continually ....

We should come to understand well
that all things are the works of the Great Spirit.
We should know that God is within all things:
the trees, the grasses,
the rivers, the mountains,
all four-legged and winged animals ....
We should come to know that the Creator
is above all these things and people.

When we understand this deeply in our hearts,
then we will all fear and love
and know the Great Spirit;
then we will be and act and live
as God intends![2]

C.S. LEWIS

1898 - 1963

Have you ever tried to check out one of the many books of C.S. Lewis at your local library? If you have, did the librarian smile and tell you about a very long waiting list for any and all of his books? This scenario is a familiar one for C.S. Lewis' regular readers as well as for those who have just discovered Lewis' work.

Born in Belfast, Northern Ireland, Clive Staples Lewis (Jack to his family and friends) was an excellent student, a clever debater, confirmed reader, and dyed-in-the-wool lover of nature. For a time he was, by his own admission, an ardent agnostic. He enlisted in the British army during World War I, and was injured in battle.

After the war, Lewis distinguished himself as a scholar, teacher, writer, wit, and conversationalist at Oxford. During these years he renewed his search for truth in religion. With intense study and the help of friends, he gradually converted from agnosticism to a firm belief in God and the teachings of Jesus Christ. As a devout and active member of the Anglican Church, he became an enthusiastic and articulate spokesperson for Christianity.

In 1954, elected to the chair of medieval and Renaissance English studies at Cambridge, Lewis felt more and more the importance of practicing what he preached. In a spirit of Christian joy, he shared his wealth with others less fortunate; he became a man of prayer, marveling at the beauty of God reflected in nature, and finding deep satisfaction in ordinary things. When his wife died less than four years after they were married, he rededicated his life to reminding others that all of us are destined for eternal life with God. What we do now will make all the difference for the future.

PRAYERS & REFLECTIONS

Challenge

Jesus warned people to "count the cost"
before becoming Christians.
"Make no mistake," he says, "if you let me,
I will make you perfect.
The moment you put yourself in my hands,
that is what you are in for."[2]

The command, "Be ye perfect,"
is not idealistic gas![2]

What's Missing?

There are persons who get so interested
in proving God's existence
that they care nothing for God himself ....
as if the good Lord had nothing to do
but exist!
And there are others so occupied
in spreading Christianity
that they have never given a thought
to Jesus Christ![3]

Each Unique Person

Each redeemed person shall forever
know and praise some one aspect of the divine beauty
better than any other creature can ....

The continually successful, yet never completed,
attempt by each soul to communicate its unique vision ...
is among the reasons for which the individual was created.[4]

Genuine Prayer

The disquieting thing is not simply
that we skimp and begrudge the duty of prayer.
The *really* disquieting thing is
that it should have to be numbered among duties at all ....
If we were perfected, prayer would not be a duty,
it would be a delight.
Someday, please God, it will be![1]

Patches of Light

Any patch of sunlight in a wood
will show you something about the sun
that you could never get from reading books on astronomy.
These pure and spontaneous pleasures
are "patches of Godlight" in the woods of our experience.[1]

Nature gives to the word *glory* a meaning for me![1]

For Worry Warts and Others

A great many people seem to think
that the mere state of being worried is itself meritorious —
I don't think it is!

We must give our own lives for others;
but even while we're doing this,
I think we're meant to *enjoy* our Lord,
and in him, our friends, our food,
our sleep, our jokes, and the birds
and the frosty sunrise.

As about the distant, so about the future.
It is very dark —
but there's always light enough
for the next step or so![5]

Praying for Others

We are often, I believe, praying for others
when we should be doing things for them.
It's so much easier to pray for a bore
than it is to go to see him![1]

The Problem of Pain

God whispers to us in our pleasures,
speaks in our conscience,
but *shouts* in our pains:
Suffering is God's megaphone to rouse a deaf world.[4]

Living the Faith

Relying on God has to begin all over again every day
as if nothing had yet been done.[1]

How little people know who think that holiness is dull.
When one meets the real thing, it is irresistible![1]

"Give us our daily bread" (not an annuity for life)
applies to spiritual gifts, too;
the little *daily* support for the *daily* trial.
Life has to be taken day by day and hour by hour.[1]

If God forgives us,
we must forgive ourselves.[1]

What God wants of us
is a cheerful insecurity.

C.S. LEWIS

Death of a Loved One

No one ever told me that grief felt so like fear.
I am not afraid, but the sensation is like being afraid.
The same fluttering in the stomach, the same restlessness ....

Meanwhile, where is God? ...
Why is God so present in our time of prosperity
and so very absent in time of trouble?

Yet I am reminded that the same thing
seems to have happened to Christ:
"My God, why have you forsaken me?"[6]

The Life of the World To Come

Then the new earth and sky, the same yet not the same as these,
will rise as we have risen in Christ.
And once again, after who knows what aeons
of silence and dark,
the birds will sing and the waters flow,
and the lights and shadows move across the hills,
and the faces of our friends will laugh upon us
with amazed recognition.

Guesses, of course, only guesses.
If they are not true, something *better* will be.
For "we know that we shall be made like God,
for we shall see him as he is"![1]

Heaven

There have been times
when I think that we do not desire heaven;
but more often I find myself wondering
whether in our heart of hearts
we have ever desired anything else![4]

38

CARYLL HOUSELANDER

1901-1954

There can be no doubt that Caryll Houselander marched to the beat of a different drummer. Friends and contemporaries of this Christian writer, artist, and activist truly loved and admired her, but readily admitted that at times she seemed somewhat eccentric and unconventional. Nevertheless, the message reflected in her day-to-day living and in her writings was consistently one of good cheer: Believe in the promises of Jesus Christ. He lives in you, and you can bring his message to others.

Born in Bath, England, Houselander was educated in convent schools and, at the age of six, was received into the Catholic Church. In the years that followed, though she had no formal training in Catholic theology, she eagerly read Scripture and studied on her own, thus developing the unusual grasp of spiritual thought reflected so well in her writings.

Houselander's personal life has been characterized as "intensely Bohemian" — at various times she earned a living writing and illustrating children's books, teaching, advertising, and woodcarving. While in her twenties, she fell in love for a time with an espionage agent, but later ended the relationship. During World War II, she worked in a censor's office and was a firewarden in wartorn London. Recognizing her own neurotic tendencies, she dedicated much of her life to working with marginalized and abused children.

The creed that Houselander wrote about and so cheerfully and prayerfully lived each day was to see Christ in others. Her firm belief in Jesus' words of farewell at the Last Supper is reflected in her writings and in her unique personality and life: "Live on in me as I do in you .... All this I tell you that my joy may be yours" (John 15:4,11).

PRAYERS & REFLECTIONS

Come, Emmanuel

Shine in us, Emmanuel,
　　Shadowless Light:
flame in us, Emmanuel,
　　Fire of Love:
burn in us, Emmanuel,
　　Morning Star:
　　　　Emmanuel.
　　God-with-us![1]

The Ultimate Acceptance

Lord,
Teach me to accept myself —
　　my own temperament,
　　my temptations,
　　my limitations,
　　my failures,
the humiliation of being myself,
　　　as I am.[1]

In Good Times and Bad

Lord,
Let us so bind ourselves
that we will not only adhere to you
　　in times of consolation,
　　in times of sweetness and devotion,
　　and when life goes smoothly,
but yet more securely —
　　in the bleak and bitter seasons of the soul,
　　in the hard iron of winters of the spirit.[1]

A Prayer for Creatures

I beseech you, be gentle!
Be gentle to the men and to the women
and to the children,
    who hold their life in their hands
    like a flower ....
Each is intent upon the flower of his own life;
for each it is the secret of his particular love —
    the joy of it and the sorrow:
    flesh and blood is consumed in it,
    like the wax of a candle consumed in flame ....
Men, women and children pass in endless procession
    and are forgotten.
We are among them.
Come, let us pray
    that the seed of our life's flowering
    fall not upon rock, fall not among thorns,
    or the hard frost or among weeds;
    but that today's sorrow
    prepare the world's soil
    and sift for sowing tomorrow.
I beseech you, be gentle!
Because when the flame is lit,
the wax is consumed quickly;
    when the leaf flowers, swift is the withering;
    but if the seed fall into the heart in fallow,
    the passing loveliness, the flicker of light —
        will remain in the dark night,
            to flower with eternal life![1]

Winter Expectations

In the dark and the cold,
    I believe in the green leaf.
In the frost and the hard crust,
    I hope in the flower.
In the cold winter, unloving,
    I love!⁴

The Terrible Everyday

"As the Father has loved me, so I have loved you" (John 15:9)

Countless millions have to make the Way of the Cross
and their way to heaven,
through the same streets,
among the same tiny circle of people,
through the same returning monotony ...

But living the Christ-life means
that we are given the power of Christ's love.
We are not only trustees of God's love for people,
entrusted to give it out second-hand —
but miraculously —
our love IS his love!²

Power-Driven

In times of need and stress,
just say again and again —
"Sacred Heart of Jesus, I place my trust in you" —
and *mean* it.
Put our Lord on his honor.
It is quite marvelous how this carries one through.
Our Lord likes to be told that you *trust* him;
he will not fail you!⁴

One Day at a Time

Self-pity reveals a void in us,
an emptiness which is the absence of God.[2]

Contrition for my weak nature
must mean looking up and seeing how forgiving,
and how *joyfully* forgiving, God is![2]

In any humble, frustrated life,
Christ may be born.[2]

We "go to Holy Communion," not because *we* want to,
but because Jesus wants to come to us.[2]

Our life in Christ is the risen life.
We live in the life of the One who has overcome death.[2]

We should open our heart very wide to joy,
should welcome it,
let it be buried deeply in us,
and wait the flowering of it with patience.[3]

JESSICA POWERS

1905-1988

During her lifelong search for truth about the relationship between the human and divine, Carmelite poet Jessica Powers found spiritual meaning in the simplest and most ordinary realities of life — the song of a robin at dusk, a soft winter snowfall, a milkweed seed moved by the wind. Each wonder of nature, she says, reveals a truth about the Creator, about joy and suffering, death and resurrection.

Born in a small farming community in Wisconsin, Jessica experienced many of the hardships and joys of rural living. Her Irish-Catholic parents were deeply religious and taught their children to value faith, family, and an honest day's work. For years, family hardships limited Jessica's educational opportunities and kept her from fulfilling her growing desire to write poetry. She was able to move to Chicago for a short time, where she worked as a clerk-typist and spent much of her free time reading, haunting libraries, and writing poetry. When her mother became gravely ill, she moved back to the family farm and took care of the Powers household.

Eventually, she returned to Chicago, and later moved to New York, where she secured child-care work with the family of noted Catholic writers and thinkers, Anton and Jessica Pegis. With their help and encouragement, she continued to write and publish poetry. Yet she knew that something was missing.

After much prayer and with counsel from a Jesuit friend, Jessica Powers joined a cloistered order of Carmelites in Milwaukee, Wisconsin. As Sister Miriam of the Holy Spirit, she found the truth she had been searching for. Although she never left her convent, she found a better way to "connect" with others and share with them her deepest religious convictions.

Song at Daybreak

This morning on the way
That yawns with light across the eastern sky
And lifts its bright arms high —
It may bring hours disconsolate or gay,
I do not know, but this much I can say:
It will be unlike any other day.

God lives in his surprise and variation.
No leaf is matched, no star is shaped to star.
No soul is like my soul in all creation
Though I may search afar.
There will be something — anguish or elation —
That is peculiar to this day alone.
I rise from sleep and say: Hail to the morning!
Come down to me, my beautiful unknown.[1]

The First Pentecost

All the apostles looked at one another;
    Words curled in the fire through the returning gloom.
    Something had changed and colored all the room.
The beauty of the Galilean mother
Took the breath from them for a little space.
    Even a cup, a chair or a brown dress
    Could draw their tears with the great loveliness
That wrote tremendous secrets every place.

That was the day when Fire came down from heaven,
    Inaugurating the first spring of love.
Blood melted in the frozen veins, and even
    The least bird sang in the mind's inmost grove.
The seed sprang into flower, and over all
Still do the multitudinous blossoms fall.[2]

Christmas Billet

Here I begin the singing
    Of my eternal song;
The deep and tender mercies
    That to the Lord belong.

At Bethlehem I intone it
    Where on a night of grace,
The music of God's mercy
    Poured over time and space.

For here the Father gave us,
    His great good will to prove,
The very Word He utters
    With everlasting love

. . . .

O Child, O carol of heaven,
    Past earth's inadequate phrase,
I take Thee, warm and living,
    To be Thyself my praise.

Oh, let my love bear witness
    Through endless ages long
How one small Word suffices!
    For an eternal song![1]

The Place of Splendor

Little one, wait.
Let me again assure you this is not the way
To gain the terminal of outer day.

Its single gate
Lies in your soul, and you must rise and go
By inward passage from what earth you know.

The steps lead down
Through valley after valley, far and far
Past the five countries where the pleasures are,

And past all known
Maps of the mind and every colored chart
And past the final outcry of the heart

. . . .

Walk till you hear
Light told in music that was never heard
And softness spoken that was not a word.

The soul grows clear
When its five senses have been fused into one:
Savor and scent and sound to splendor run.

The smothered roar
Of the eternities, their vast unrest
And infinite peace are deep in your own breast.

That light-swept shore
Will shame the data of grief upon your scroll.
Child, have none told you? *God* is in your soul.[1]

If You Have Nothing

The gesture of a gift is adequate.
If you have nothing: laurel leaf nor bay,
No flower, no seed, no apple gathered late,
Do not in desperation lay
The beauty of your tears upon the clay.

No gift is proper to a Deity.
No fruit is worthy for such power to bless.
If you have nothing, gather back your sigh,
And with your hands held high,
Your heart held high,
Lift up your emptiness![1]

The Thought of Death

There is no place on earth where I can hide
From death or the thought of death.
Therefore I have prepared my house to receive him.

I have set slim gold candles in the windows,
And I have spread a blue velvet carpet
For his white feet.

I have talked to him in the sea and wind and stars
And in the faces of those I love;
And he has answered me.[2]

ANNE MORROW LINDBERGH

1907 - 1993

I n what is probably her best-known and best-loved book, *Gift from the Sea,* Anne Morrow Lindbergh stressed the human need for get-away times for quiet, peaceful reflection: "Only when one is connected to one's own core is one connected to others .... and, for me, the core, the inner spring, can best be refound through solitude." During her eventful and often hectic life, she learned firsthand of her need to set aside special times to turn to God, to focus on what is really important, to let go of the "small stuff," and return to loved ones and her daily routine, renewed, refreshed, and ready-to-go.

Born into an upper middle-class family in Englewood, New Jersey, Anne Morrow enjoyed the good life — prep schools, summer vacations in Maine, travels abroad. Despite the abundance of material possessions, however, religion was of prime importance in the Morrow household. Influenced by their Puritan roots, Anne's parents raised their children to be devout and prayerful Presbyterians.

In 1927, Anne met "Lucky Lindy," Charles A. Lindbergh, recently returned from his historic transatlantic flight. They fell in love and were married within two years. After Anne learned to fly and to navigate a plane, she accompanied her husband on flights through-out the world. Her career as a writer blossomed. Despite their constant "busy-ness" and much unwanted publicity, the couple kept their growing family a top priority. Throughout their lives of fulfillment and tragedy, of fame and longings for privacy, Anne and Charles stayed well-grounded. Anne Morrow Lindbergh often said that it was their faith and their prayer-filled lives that carried them through.

PRAYERS & REFLECTIONS

The Living Bread

"I myself am the living bread come down from heaven" (John 6:51).

The living bread that Jesus speaks of ...
can be divided endlessly and still nourish,
like the miracle of the loaves and fishes.
The bread of love!
Only love can be divided endlessly and still not diminish.[1]

The "Stuff" of Living

To appreciate life, we must take it at all its levels:
at its top crust, its middle everyday layer,
and then at some deeper core ...
felt once or twice at great moments.

Most people get only the middle layer;
children always get the crust;
but very few people reach the inner core.
Saints perhaps and great artists ....
The rest of people feel it once or twice in their lives —
when they're in love, sharpened by pain or sorrow,
or near death.[2]

Here and Now

Security in a relationship lies neither in looking back
to what was in nostalgia,
nor what it might be in dread or anticipation —
but living in the present relationship
and accepting it as it is *now.*[3]

Time Alone

We are solitary.
We may delude ourselves and act as though this is not so.
We seem so frightened today of being alone
that we never let it happen.
Yet, there is a quality of being alone
that is incredibly precious.
Life rushes back into the void —
richer, more vivid, fuller than before.[3]

Listening

When Christ said, "Love one another ..."
maybe he meant *listen* to one another;
listen to your enemy, listen to your neighbor,
listen to your children ....[1]

Great with Life

The phrase "pregnant woman" cheapens life,
for it leaves out the child ....
The Bible says it better —
"Mary, great with child."
That is it — *great* with life ....
What a gift — what a trust —
this gift of a child, of life![2]

Afraid in the Waiting Room

It is only the waiting room of death
that can make us fearful,
and not the room of death itself —
not when we open that inner door
and stand in the holy of holies![2]

Getting Down to Basics

Joy warms us; fear makes us cold.

We partake of God's love
when we love one another.

If we had an hour of contemplation at home,
we might be readier to give ourselves at church!

People die all the time in their lives.
Parts of them die when they make
the wrong kinds of decisions —
decisions against life.

Nearness to death makes life more alive
and beauty more beautiful.

Apollo 8 — December, 1968

Radiating light over the heavens,
it seems to be the focus of the world,
as the star of Bethlehem once was
on another December night centuries ago.
    But what does it promise?
        What new world?
    What hope for mortals struggling on earth?

We have been given another image of ourselves
    and our place in the cosmos ....
Other generations will judge what has changed,
what is born and what is promised ....
Along with a new sense of earth's smallness,
    a fragile, shining ball floating in space,
we have a new sense of earth's richness and beauty ....

We begin to realize how utterly we are earth's children.
Perhaps now we can accept our responsibility to earth,
    and our heritage from it,
        which we must protect if we are to survive![4]

THOMAS MERTON

1915 - 1968

The life story and numerous writings of Thomas Merton, Trappist priest-poet-philosopher, have been and continue to be major influences in the lives of countless individuals searching for truth and meaning in their lives. His account of his own conversion to Catholicism and vocation to the priesthood is told in the 1948 book, *The Seven Storey Mountain.*

Born in France of parents who were world travelers, Merton lived and went to school in various places — France, New York, Bermuda, England. During his school years, the young atheist questioned everything, lived riotously, and answered to no one. But gradually his readings and the help of friends led him to search and pray and, in 1938, to enter the Catholic Church.

During the next years, Merton accepted a teaching position at St. Bonaventure College in New York and, for a time, thought of becoming involved in the social programs of Baroness Catherine de Hueck. Instead, in 1941, after much prayer and soul-searching, he entered the Trappist monastery of Gethsemani in Kentucky. His next years were spent adapting to an austere life-style, writing and publishing spiritual works, preparing for the priesthood, developing an interest in Eastern spirituality and various social concerns, looking for more times of solitude, yet traveling and lecturing frequently.

Persons attracted to and influenced by Thomas Merton and his works were shocked to learn of his sudden and untimely death in Bangkok in 1968. Perhaps today's loyal friends and readers can be comforted by a promise Merton made years ago: "My readers have given me a gift of friendship and love which is precious to me beyond estimation .... Let me assure them of my gratitude, my love, and my prayers .... I hope we will be together in Paradise."

PRAYERS & REFLECTIONS

Sounds of Silence

God our Father,
    I beg you to keep me in this silence
    so that I may learn from it
        the word of your peace,
        the word of your mercy, and
        the word of your gentleness to the world:
    that through me your word may be heard
    where it has not been possible for anyone to hear it
                for a long time.[2]

Great Expectations

Upon our hope ... depends the great liberty of the whole universe.
Because our hope is the pledge of a new heaven and a new earth,
in which all things will be what they were meant to be.
They will rise, together with us, in Christ.
The beasts and the trees will one day share with us a new
creation, and we will see them as God sees them and know
that they are very good.[1]

Blueprint for Happiness

True happiness is found in unselfish love,
a love which increases in proportion as it is shared.
There is no end to the sharing of love, and, therefore,
the potential happiness of such love is without limit.[1]

On the Way

We are living in a world that is absolutely transparent;
    God is shining through all the time![2]

God loves you
    or you wouldn't be.[4]

Let go and become
    who you always have been.[4]

It was because the saints loved God
    that they loved everybody.[4]

True hope is trusting that
    what we have, where we are, and who we are
    is more than enough for us as creatures of God.[4]

Prayer: The Ultimate Communication

All true prayer somehow confesses
our absolute dependence on the Lord of life and death.[1]

We make ourselves what we are
by the way we address God.[1]

Since the main reason for our existence
is the knowledge and love of God,
when our conscious contact with God is severed,
we sleep or we die.[1]

The Big Picture

What are the horizons that lie ahead
in our ascent to the City of God in heaven?
There are peaks before us now,
serene with snow and light,
above the level of the tempest.
They are far away.
We almost never see them — they are so high.
But we lift up our eyes toward them,
for there the saints dwell:
and these are the mountains of holiness
whence cometh our help.[3]

By nature and temperament, Bishop Oscar Romero was very shy and reserved, slow to act, slow to accept change. With God's help and fervent prayer, this mild-mannered priest became a fearless, decisive, and outspoken man of action, defending the poor and oppressed people of El Salvador.

Born in a tiny village in El Salvador, Romero always felt drawn to the priesthood and, at thirteen, entered the minor seminary in San Salvador. Because he was an excellent student and was well-grounded in his vocation, he was sent to Rome to study theology. After ordination in 1942, he returned to El Salvador and was appointed secretary to the bishop of San Miguel. There, for the next twenty-three years, Father Romero earned recognition as a pastor, editor of the diocesan newspaper, radio preacher, and promoter of various conservative lay organizations. Later he was made auxiliary bishop of San Salvador.

In 1974, Romero was appointed bishop of a small rural diocese and became increasingly aware of the outrageous injustices suffered by the peasant classes at the hands of wealthy landowners and the military. In the years that followed, he became a tireless champion of the "poor and the powerless." Later, as archbishop of San Salvador, he spoke out daily, using the pulpit, radio broadcasts, and the archdiocesan newspaper to condemn tyranny and oppression. Finally, tired of his persistence, rightist oppressors gunned down Romero as he celebrated Mass in a hospital chapel.

In 1942, Father Romero's ordination holy card had read: "May this sacrifice please you, O Lord." There can be no doubt that the soft-spoken priest's life and ultimate sacrifice had indeed been very pleasing to the Lord.

PRAYERS & REFLECTIONS

Christianity Is a Person

Christianity is not a collection
of truths to be believed, of laws to be obeyed ....
Christianity is a *person,*
one who loved us very much,
one who calls for our love.
Christianity is Jesus Christ!

Follow Me!

"If anyone wishes to come after me, he must deny his very self,
take up his cross, and follow in my steps" (Mark 8:34).

We must learn the invitation of Christ.
Those who wish to come after him
must renounce themselves ....
and follow the mind of Christ,
which can lead to death,
but will also surely lead to resurrection.[1]

To be a Christian means to have the courage
to preach the true meaning of Christ
and not to be afraid, not to be silent out of fear ....
To be a Christian means to have the courage
given by the Holy Spirit ...
to be a valiant soldier for Christ,
and to make his teaching prevail.[1]

Getting Out the Message

God's best microphone is Christ,
and Christ's best microphone is the Church,
and the Church is all of you![1]

The Violence of Love

"They shall beat their swords into plowshares" (Isaiah 2:4).

The violence we preach is not
the violence of sword, the violence of hatred.
It is the violence of love, of brotherhood —
the violence that wills to beat weapons
into sickles for work.[1]

Mary Shows the Way

Even when all despaired
at the hours when Christ was dying on the cross,
Mary, serene, awaited the hour of the resurrection.
Mary is the symbol of people who suffer
oppression and injustice.
Theirs is the calm suffering that awaits the resurrection.[1]

Ready to Greet the Day

When we leave Mass, we ought to go out
the way Moses descended Mount Sinai:
with his face shining,
with his heart brave and strong,
ready to face the world's difficulties![1]

Feeling Alone

"My God, my God, why have you forsaken me?"
(Matthew 27:46)

It is the psychology of suffering to feel alone,
to feel that no one understands, to feel forsaken ....
But God is closer to us
when we think he is far away and doesn't hear us ....
We need to understand that God
not only gives happiness but also tests our faithfulness
in moments of affliction.
It is then that prayer and religion have most merit:
when we are faithful
in spite of not feeling the Lord's presence.[1]

Facing Death

Though I fear a violent death ...
I know that I must hand my life over to God
regardless of the way it may end:
I believe that, with God's grace,
I can face any unknown circumstances ....
but I also believe that more valiant than surrender in death
is the surrender of one's whole life —
a life lived for God![2]

The Deepest Joy the Heart Can Have

It is wrong to be sad.
Christians cannot be pessimists —
we must always nourish in our hearts
the fullness of joy.
Try it, brothers and sisters!

I have tried it many times,
and in the darkest moments ...
to unite myself intimately
with Christ my friend,
and to feel a comfort
that all the joys of earth do not give —
the joy of feeling close to God.
It is the deepest joy the heart can have![1]

HENRI J.M. NOUWEN

1932 - 1996

Henri Nouwen was a man on the go. As preacher and teacher, lecturer and writer, contemplative and activist, this tireless man of God challenged others to join him in his continual search for truth about what it means to live and die as a true Christian.

Born before World War II in Nijkerk, Holland, Nouwen was raised in a staunchly Catholic family. Often harassed during the war by German occupying troops, his parents did all they could to foster and maintain a prayerful Christian atmosphere in their home. After the war, Henri entered the local seminary, continued his studies in Utrecht, and was ordained in 1957. In the years that followed, he studied and taught psychology and pastoral theology at various colleges and universities in Holland, Rome, and the United States.

Always "pastoral," Father Nouwen spent much time and energy working among the poor in South and Central America and with the mentally impaired in Toronto, Canada. He also studied firsthand the problems of aging and developed some comforting thoughts on a process shared by all of us. He wrote an incredible number of books and articles on spirituality and ministry, and became a much sought-after preacher, teacher, and lecturer.

Father Nouwen's work was flourishing in 1996 when he learned that his good friend Cardinal Joseph Bernardin of Chicago was gravely ill. Cardinal Bernardin writes, in his final book, *The Gift of Peace,* that Nouwen took time out in July, 1996, to visit the dying man and to remind him that "death is a friend rather than an enemy." Less than two months later, Father Nouwen died of a heart attack. Before Bernardin himself died in November, he wrote of his friend: "There is no doubt that he (Nouwen) was prepared. He spent his lifetime teaching others how to live and how to die."

PRAYERS & REFLECTIONS

To the God of Ebb and Flow

Dear Lord,
    Although I experience many ups and downs
        in my emotions,
    and often feel great shifts and changes
        in my inner life,
                you remain the same ....
    There are days of sadness and days of joy;
    there are feelings of guilt and feelings of gratitude;
    there are moments of failure and moments of success;
        but all of them are embraced
        by your unwavering love ....
O Lord, sea of love and goodness,
    Let me not fear too much the storms and winds
        of my daily life;
    and let me know that there is ebb and flow,
    but that the sea remains the same. Amen.[1]

Blessed Are the Peacemakers!

Christ is the first peacemaker
since he opened the house of God to all people
and thus made the old creation new.
We are sent to this world to be peacemakers in his name.

We cannot love issues, but we can love people —
and the love of people reveals to us
the way to deal with issues!

To Jesus, My Inspiration, My Friend

Dear Lord,

Help me to keep my eyes on you.

You are the incarnation of divine love;

you are the expression of God's infinite compassion;

you are the visible manifestation

of the Father's holiness;

you are beauty, goodness, forgiveness, and mercy.

In you all can be found ...

you have the words of eternal life;

you are food and drink;

you are the Way, the Truth, and the Life ...

In and through you, I can see and find my way

to the heavenly Father.

O Holy One,

Be all to me.

You are my Lord, my Savior, my Redeemer, my Guide,

my Consoler, my Comforter, my Hope,

my Joy and my Peace.

To you I want to give all that I am.

Let me be generous, not stingy or hesitant.

Let me give you all —

all that I have, think, do, and feel.

It is yours, O Lord —

Please accept it and make it fully your own. Amen.[1]

Pray with Hope!

Hope expects the coming of something new.
Hope looks ahead toward that which is not yet.
Hope accepts and risks the unspecified.

When you pray with hope,
   you turn yourself toward a God
   who can be trusted unconditionally!
It is enough to know that God is a *faithful* God.[5]

Never Alone in Our Suffering

There can be no human beings
who are completely alone in their sufferings
since God, in and through Jesus,
has become Emmanuel, God with us.

It belongs to the center of our faith
that God is a faithful God
who does not want us ever to be alone ....

The Good News of the Gospel, therefore,
is not that God came to take our suffering away,
but that God wanted to become a part of it!

Getting Older

To care for the aging means, first of all,
to enter into close contact with your own aging self,
to sense your own time,
and to experience the movements of your own life cycle.
From this aging self, healing can come forth,
and others can be invited to cast off
the paralyzing fear for their future.[4]

Ministry

Ministry means the ongoing attempt
to put one's own search for God,
with all the moments of pain, joy, despair and hope,
at the disposal of those who want to join this search
but do not know how.[2]

We need each other
and are able to give each other
much more than we often realize.[3]

Reality Check

It seems indeed important that we face death
before we are in any real danger of dying —
and reflect on our mortality
before all our conscious and unconscious energy
is directed to the struggle to survive.[4]

KATHLEEN NORRIS

1947 -

I t seems an unlikely scenario — a successful poet-author, happily married woman, devout Presbyterian, and worldly-wise baby boomer — as a deeply involved and dedicated Benedictine oblate. Yet such is the case with best-selling author Kathleen Norris, who has told her unusual story in two books, *Dakota: A Spiritual Geography* and *The Cloister Walk.*

Norris explains in *Dakota* that more than twenty years ago she and her husband, poet David Dwyer, left their home and the hectic pace of life in New York so that she could begin a search for her religious heritage, and so that both of them could explore the possibilities of a more peaceful and serene life on the Great Plains. Thus it was that they moved to Lemmon, South Dakota, into the very house built by her grandparents many years before. Their move was to be one that would change their lives forever.

Though she had drifted away from church-going, Norris felt the need to examine the values and faith experiences of family members and to find her own way to God. She began attending and participating in Presbyterian services and became involved in various ministries in the area. What she had not anticipated during her ongoing faith search was an accidental encounter with some Benedictines and their way of life while she was attending a cultural event in North Dakota.

From that first meeting, Norris was drawn to Benedictine spirituality: daily Scripture readings, special times of prayer and silence, respect for the seasons and times of the day, and the spirit of community and hospitality. After some time, with consultation with her husband and family members, and with much thought and prayer, Kathleen Norris decided to become a Benedictine oblate (associate), that is, to live monastic ideals in very special ways. Yet her life as a loving wife, active Presbyterian, community-minded citizen, and thoughtful writer has continued. With good humor, Norris recently summed up her faith identity: "This is who I am: a complete Protestant with a decidedly ecumenical bent."

PRAYERS & REFLECTIONS

The Companionable Dark

... Not the easy dark
of dusk and candles,
but the dark from which comforts flee.
The deep down dark
of one by one,
dark of wind
and dust, dark in which stars burn.
The floodwater dark
of hope, Jesus in agony
in the garden, Esther pacing
her bitter palace. A dark
by which we see, dark like truth,
like flesh on bone:
Help me, who am alone,
and have no help but thee.[1]

The Desert Can Teach Us

... It is the desert's grimness,
its stillness and isolation,
that can bring us back to love.
Here we discover the paradox of the
contemplative life:
that the desert of solitude
can be the school where we learn to love others![2]

Wash Day

Hanging up wet clothes
gives me time alone under the sky
to think, to grieve —
and gathering the clean clothes in,
smelling the sunlight on them,
is victory![2]

Advent: Waiting and Wondering

Preaching in both a town and a country church,
I found that the hard texts of Advent —
texts about waiting, about judgment, and last things —
were accepted in the country
while in the town there was already pressure
to start celebrating Christmas.[2]

Risky Business

The radical hope we must place in others ...
reminds me of Jesus,
who called disciples from their ordinary work
to change the world
without once consulting a personnel manager
to determine if they had the aptitude or credentials
for the job.[2]

Hospitality

I have become convinced
that hospitality is at the center
of the Christian faith —
the bread of the Eucharist is called the "host," after all,
and with good reason.[3]

Good Friday

It is the morning after, the coming-to.
Last night we feasted with our dearest friends,
and now we wake to find
that for the dearest of them, Jesus himself,
death is imminent.[3]

Needed: Good Listeners

Listening is often the major part of ministry:
people in a crisis need to tell their story
from beginning to end,
and the best thing — often the only thing —
that you can do is to sit there and take it in.[3]

Christian Inheritance

It is my Christian inheritance
that largely defines me.[2]

Disconnecting from change does not recapture the past.
It loses the future.[2]

Conversion means starting with who we are,
not who we wish we were.[2]

Silence is the best response to mystery.[2]

A moment of rest,
noon prayer is like a door opening into afternoon and evening.[3]

Repentance is valuable
because it opens in us the idea of change.[3]

ACKNOWLEDGMENTS

Numbers listed below correspond with those used throughout the book and indicate the source from which an excerpt was taken.

Acknowledgments

Wm. B. Eerdmans Publishing Co., Grand Rapids, MI. *The Communion of Saints* ©1990. See Patrick of Ireland and Thomas More. Reprinted with permission. All rights reserved.

Patrick of Ireland

[1] *The Living Legend of St. Patrick* ©1990 by Alannah Hopkin. St. Martin's Press, Inc., New York. Reprinted with permission. All rights reserved.

[2] *The Communion of Saints.*

Clare of Assisi

[1] *Clare, Her Light and Her Song* by Karen Kerper. ©1984 Franciscan Press, Quincy, IL. Reprinted with permission. All rights reserved.

Thomas More

[1] *The Communion of Saints.*

[2] *Thomas More: The Search for the Inner Man* by Louis L. Martz. ©1990 Yale University Press, New Haven, CT. Reprinted with permission. All rights reserved.

Mary Theresa of Jesus Gerhardinger

[1] *Trust and Dare* ©1985, edited by the School Sisters of Notre Dame General Council, Rome. Inland Press, Menomonee Falls, WI. Reprinted with permission.

[2] *SSND Papers* by Mary Theresa of Jesus Gerhardinger, Nos. 714, 949, 778, 774, 118, 5327, 2534, 29, 3. Reprinted with permission.

ACKNOWLEDGMENTS

Black Elk

[1]*Black Elk Speaks* by John G. Neihardt. ©1932, 1959, 1972 University of Nebraska Press, Lincoln, NE. Reprinted with permission. All rights reserved.

[2]*The Sacred Pipe*, recorded and edited by Joseph Epes Brown. ©1953 by University of Oklahoma Press, Publishing Division, Norman, OK. Used with permission. All rights reserved.

C. S. Lewis

[1]*Letters to Malcolm: Chiefly on Prayer* by C. S. Lewis. ©1964, 1963 by C. S. Lewis PTE Ltd. and renewed 1992, 1991 by Arthur Owen Barfield. Reprinted by permission of Harcourt Brace & Company.

[2]*Mere Christianity* ©1943, 1945, 1952; [3]*The Great Divorce* ©1984, 1946; [4]*The Problem of Pain* ©1944 by C. S. Lewis. Reprinted with permission of HarperCollins, Ltd., Hammersmith, London, United Kingdom.

[5]Extract from *Letter to Dom Bede Griffiths of December 4, 1946.* ©1981 C. S. Lewis Pte. Ltd., reproduced with permission of Curtis Brown Limited, London.

[6]*A Grief Observed* ©1989 by C. S. Lewis. Reprinted with permission of HarperCollins, New York.

Caryll Houselander

[1]*The Flowering Tree* ©1945; [2]*Passion of the Infant Christ* ©1949; [3]*The Reed of God* ©1944. All by Caryll Houselander. [4]*The Letters of Caryll Houselander* by Maisie Ward Sheed ©1965. All reprinted by permission of Sheed and Ward, 115 E. Armour Blvd., Kansas City, MO 64141. All rights reserved.

Jessica Powers

Excerpts from the following books written by Jessica Powers are reprinted with permission of the Carmelite Monastery, Pewaukee, WI. All rights reserved.

[1]*The Place of Splendor* ©1946; [2]*The Lantern Burns* ©1929.

Anne Morrow Lindbergh

[1]*Dearly Beloved: A Theme and Variations* by Anne Morrow Lindbergh ©1962 Harcourt Brace & Company and renewed 1990 by Anne Morrow Lindbergh. Reprinted with permission of the publisher.

[2]*The Steep Ascent* ©1944 and renewed 1971 by Anne Morrow Lindbergh. Reprinted by permission of Harcourt Brace & Company.

[3]*Gift from the Sea* ©1955 Random House, Inc. (or any of its subsidiaries) New York. Reprinted with permission.

[4]*Earth Shine* by Anne Morrow Lindbergh. ©1969 Harcourt Brace, & Company. Reprinted with permission of Reeve Lindbergh.

Thomas Merton

[1]*No Man Is An Island* by Thomas Merton. ©1955 The Abbey of Our Lady of Gethsemani and renewed 1983 by the Trustees of the Thomas Merton Legacy Trust. Reprinted with permission of Harcourt Brace & Company.

[2]*A Retreat with Thomas Merton* by M. Basil Pennington ©1991. Reprinted with permission of the Continuum Publishing Company, New York.

[3]*Bread in the Wilderness* by Thomas Merton. ©1953 The Order of St. Benedict, Inc. Published by The Liturgical Press, Collegeville, MN. Reprinted with permision.

[4]Various sources. Reprinted with permission of the Merton Legacy Trust.

Oscar Romero

[1]*The Church Is All of You* by Oscar Romero. Compiled and translated by James R. Brochman, S.J. ©1984 Chicago Province of the Society of Jesus. Reprinted with permission of HarperCollins, New York.

[2]*Archbishop Romero — Memories and Reflections* by Jon Sobrino. ©1990 Orbis Books, Maryknoll, NY. Reprinted with permission.

ACKNOWLEDGMENTS

Henri J. M. Nouwen

Excerpts from the following four books by Henri Nouwen are reprinted with permission of Doubleday, a division of Bantam Doubleday Dell Publishing Group, Inc., New York. All rights reserved. [1]*A Cry for Mercy: Prayers from the Genesee* ©1981; [2]*Creative Ministry: Beyond Professionalism in Teaching, Preaching, Counseling, Organizing and Celebrating* ©1971; [3]*Clowning in Rome* ©1979; [4]*Aging: the Fulfillment of Life* ©1974.

[5]*With Open Hands* by Henri Nouwen. ©1972 Ave Maria Press, Notre Dame, IN. Used with permission of the publisher. All rights reserved.

Kathleen Norris

[1]"The Companionable Dark" (second stanza) from *Little Girls in Church* by Kathleen Norris ©1995. Reprinted with permission of the University of Pittsburgh Press, Pittsburgh, PA. All rights reserved.

[2]*Dakota: A Spiritual Geography* ©1993 by Kathleen Norris. Excerpts reprinted by permission of Ticknor & Fields/Houghton Mifflin Co., New York. All rights reserved.

[3]*The Cloister Walk* ©1996 by Kathleen Norris. Excerpts reprinted by permission of Riverhead Books, a division of The Putnam Publishing Group, New York.